Phillips

GW00391245

Lang**Syne**
PUBLISHING
WRITING *to* REMEMBER

Lang**Syne**

PUBLISHING

WRITING *to* REMEMBER

79 Main Street, Newtongrange,
Midlothian EH22 4NA
Tel: 0131 344 0414
E-mail: info@lang-syne.co.uk
www.langsyneshop.co.uk

Design by Dorothy Meikle
Printed by Printwell Ltd
© Lang Syne Publishers Ltd 2022

ISBN 978-1-85217-472-9

Phillips

MOTTO:
Patriotism leads me
(and)
In our inner mind, we know what is right.

CREST:
An arm with the hand holding a broken spear
(and)
A demi-lion rampant.

NAME variations include:
Phelps
Philp
Philips
Philipson
Phillipson
Phillip
Phipps

Chapter one:

The origins of popular surnames

by George Forbes and Iain Gray

If you don't know where you came from, you won't know where you're going is a frequently quoted observation and one that has a particular resonance today when there has been a marked upsurge in interest in genealogy, with increasing numbers of people curious to trace their family roots.

Main sources for genealogical research include census returns and official records of births, marriages and deaths – and the key to unlocking the detail they contain is obviously a family surname, one that has been 'inherited' and passed from generation to generation.

No matter our station in life, we all have a surname – but it was not until about the middle of the fourteenth century that the practice of being identified by a particular surname became commonly established throughout the British Isles.

Previous to this, it was normal for a person to be identified through the use of only a forename.

But as population gradually increased and there were many more people with the same forename, surnames were adopted to distinguish one person, or community, from another.

Many common English surnames are patronymic in origin, meaning they stem from the forename of one's father – with 'Johnson,' for example, indicating 'son of John.'

It was the Normans, in the wake of their eleventh century conquest of Anglo-Saxon England, a pivotal moment in the nation's history, who first brought surnames into usage – although it was a gradual process.

For the Normans, these were names initially based on the title of their estates, local villages and chateaux in France to distinguish and identify these landholdings.

Such grand descriptions also helped enhance the prestige of these warlords and generally glorify their lofty positions high above the humble serfs slaving away below in the pecking order who had only single names, often with Biblical connotations as in Pierre and Jacques.

The only descriptive distinctions among the peasantry concerned their occupations, like 'Pierre the swineherd' or 'Jacques the ferryman.'

Roots of surnames that came into usage in England not only included Norman-French, but also Old French, Old Norse, Old English, Middle English, German, Latin, Greek, Hebrew and the Gaelic languages of the Celts.

The Normans themselves were originally Vikings, or 'Northmen', who raided, colonised and eventually settled down around the French coastline.

They had sailed up the Seine in their long-boats in 900AD under their ferocious leader Rollo and ruled the roost in north eastern France before sailing over to conquer England in 1066 under Duke William of Normandy – better known to posterity as William the Conqueror, or King William I of England.

Granted lands in the newly-conquered England, some of their descendants later acquired territories in Wales, Scotland and Ireland – taking not only their own surnames, but also the practice of adopting a surname, with them.

But it was in England where Norman rule and custom first impacted, particularly in relation to the adoption of surnames.

This is reflected in the famous *Domesday Book*, a massive survey of much of England and Wales, ordered by William I, to determine who owned what, what it was worth and therefore how much they were liable to pay in taxes to the voracious Royal Exchequer.

Completed in 1086 and now held in the National Archives in Kew, London, 'Domesday' was an Old English word meaning 'Day of Judgement.'

This was because, in the words of one contemporary chronicler, "its decisions, like those of the Last Judgement, are unalterable."

It had been a requirement of all those English landholders – from the richest to the poorest – that they identify themselves for the purposes of the survey and for future reference by means of a surname.

This is why the *Domesday Book*, although written in Latin as was the practice for several centuries with both civic and ecclesiastical records, is an invaluable source for the early appearance of a wide range of English surnames.

Several of these names were coined in connection with occupations.

These include Baker and Smith, while Cooks, Chamberlains, Constables and Porters were to be found carrying out duties in large medieval households.

The church's influence can be found in names such as Bishop, Friar and Monk while the popular name of Bennett derives from the late fifth to mid-sixth century Saint Benedict, founder of the Benedictine order of monks.

The early medical profession is represented by Barber, while businessmen produced names that include Merchant and Sellers.

Down at the village watermill, the names that cropped up included Millar/Miller, Walker and Fuller, while other self-explanatory trades included Cooper, Tailor, Mason and Wright.

Even the scenery was utilised as in Moor, Hill, Wood and Forrest while the hunt and the chase supplied names that include Hunter, Falconer, Fowler and Fox.

Colours are also a source of popular surnames, as in Black, Brown, Gray/Grey, Green and White, and would have denoted the colour of the clothing the person habitually wore or, apart from the obvious exception of 'Green', one's hair colouring or even complexion.

The surname Red developed into Reid, while

Blue was rare and no-one wanted to be associated with yellow.

Rather self-important individuals took surnames that include Goodman and Wiseman, while physical attributes crept into surnames such as Small and Little.

Many families proudly boast the heraldic device known as a Coat of Arms, as featured on our front cover.

The central motif of the Coat of Arms would originally have been what was borne on the shield of a warrior to distinguish himself from others on the battlefield.

Not featured on the Coat of Arms, but high-lighted on page three, is the family motto and related crest – with the latter frequently different from the central motif.

Adding further variety to the rich cultural heritage that is represented by surnames is the appearance in recent times in lists of the 100 most common names found in England of ones that include Khan, Patel and Singh – names that have proud roots in the vast sub-continent of India.

Echoes of a far distant past can still be found in our surnames and they can be borne with pride in commemoration of our forebears.

Chapter two:

Dark Ages

A name derived from that of an ancient Greek warrior king, 'Phillips' has a number of equally popular spelling variants that include Philip, Phillip, Phelps, Philipson and Phillipson.

The Greek king was Philip II of Macedon, father of Alexander the Great and who ruled from 359 BC until he was assassinated by one of his bodyguards in 336 BC.

'Phillips' denotes 'son of Phillip', and derives from the Greek *philippus* – meaning 'friend of horses' or 'lover of horses' and also descriptive of a skilled horseman.

Although earliest records of the name in the British Isles appear in the modern day English county of Kent – known as 'the garden of England' – it is particularly identified with Wales.

The reasons for this lie far back through the dim mists of time – and some bearers of the name today may well trace an ancestry that goes as far back as the ancient Britons.

Also known as the Brythons, or British, they

were a Celtic race whose golden age was from the British Iron Age to the Early Middle Ages.

Their domain stretched from throughout present day England to as far north as the Firth of Forth, in present day Scotland.

Following the Roman conquest of 43 AD, their culture gradually blended with that of the Romans to form Romano-British culture.

A very early family of bearers of the Phillips name found in Kent traced a descent, during the Romano-British era, from Magnus Maximus, Western Roman Emperor from 383 AD to 388 AD.

Known grandly in Latin as Flavius Magnus Maximus Augustus, it was as an already distinguished Roman Army general that he was posted to Britain in 380 AD.

Responsible for repelling an invasion of Picts and Scots, he usurped the Imperial Throne against Emperor Gratian and was proclaimed emperor by his troops in 383.

Legend holds that Maximus was also declared 'King of Britain' following his marriage to a daughter of Octavius, then King of the Britons.

Intriguingly, Maximus figures prominently in the earliest Welsh genealogies – not only as an ancestor of some of those who became bearers of the Phillips name, but also as the founder of a number of Welsh dynastic kingdoms.

Known in Welsh as *Maesen Wiedig* or *Maxen Wledig*, he died in Rome in 388 AD after having earlier departed British shores for Gaul.

According to the sixth century British cleric and historian Gildas, before Maximus departed he had transferred power to local rulers who, in Wales, established several royal dynasties.

It is perhaps through this that some historical sources site him as having been the 'father' of the Welsh nation.

His name appears in lists of what are known as *The Fifteen Tribes of Wales*, and is inscribed on the stone pillar known as the Pillar of Eliseg.

Erected by Cyngen ap Cadell, King of Powys, about 500 years after Maximus departed Britain, it is located near Valle Crucis Abbey, Denbighshire.

Known in Welsh as the *Croes Elisedd*, it was partially destroyed by Parliamentary forces during the seventeenth century English Civil War, but was re-erected in 1779 and remains a major tourist attraction.

In the chaotic decade following the withdrawal of the last of the Roman legions from Britain in 406 AD, the period known as the Dark Ages descended on the island.

This was through those Germanic tribes who invaded and settled in the south and east of the island of Britain from about the early fifth century.

Known as the Anglo-Saxons, or Saxons, they were composed of the Jutes, from the area of the Jutland Peninsula in modern Denmark, the Saxons from Lower Saxony, in modern Germany and the Angles from the Angeln area of Germany.

It was the Angles who gave the name 'Engla land', or 'Aengla land' – better known as 'England.'

It was during the Anglo-Saxon onslaught on Britain that the legendary and celebrated figure of King Arthur appears.

Nothing is known with any degree of certainty about this great figure of early British history, but he is reputed to have fought twelve ferocious battles against the Saxons as 'war leader' of the native British, including the 515 AD battle of Mount Badon.

Killed in battle, this 'once and future king' is nevertheless according to legend slumbering somewhere in a mountain fastness awaiting the call to restore his people to their rightful dominion over the land.

The Saxons held sway in what became England from approximately 550 AD to 1066, with the main kingdoms those of Sussex, Wessex, Northumbria, Mercia, Kent, East Anglia and Essex.

Whoever controlled the most powerful of these kingdoms was tacitly recognised as overall 'king' – one of the most noted being Alfred the Great, King of Wessex from 871 to 899.

It was during his reign that the famous *Anglo-Saxon Chronicle* was compiled – an invaluable source of Anglo-Saxon history – while Alfred was designated in early documents as *Rex Anglorum Saxonum*, King of the English Saxons.

Other important Anglo-Saxon works include the epic *Beowulf* and the seventh century *Caedmon's Hymn*.

Through the Anglo-Saxons, the Brythonic language of Britons such as those who came to bear the Phillips name was gradually replaced by Old English, which transformed from the eleventh century onwards into Middle English.

The Anglo-Saxons, who had usurped the

power of indigenous Britons such as the ancestors of those who would later bear the Phillips name, – were referred by them as 'Saeson' or 'Saxones.'

It is from this that the Scottish-Gaelic term for 'English people' of 'Sasannach' derives, the Irish-Gaelic 'Sasanach' and the Welsh 'Saeson.'

We learn from the *Anglo-Saxon Chronicle* how the religion of the early Anglo-Saxons was one that pre-dated the establishment of Christianity in the British Isles.

Known as a form of Germanic paganism, with roots in Old Norse religion, it shared much in common with the Druidic 'nature-worshipping' religion of the indigenous Britons.

It was in the closing years of the sixth century that Christianity began to take a hold in Britain, while by approximately 690 it had become the 'established' religion of Anglo-Saxon England.

The ancestors of many of today's bearers of the Phillips name found themselves pushed by the Saxons from their heartland of Kent into what is now modern day Wales.

This is why the Phillips name is entwined with the histories of both England and Wales.

In Wales, one of their noted ancestors was

Rhodri Mawr, also known as Rhodri ap Merfyn, but better known as Rhodri the Great and reputed to have been a descendant of Magnus Maximus.

Born in about 820 AD, of the Welsh royal houses of Gwynedd and Powys, he inherited the kingdom of Gwynedd on his father's death in 844 AD.

Later inheriting the kingdoms of Powys and Seisyllwg, he came to rule practically all of Wales.

Battling with the Saxons and the Vikings, he defeated a Viking Army under Gorm in 856 AD, while twenty years later he engaged in battle with them again on Anglesey.

It was about a year after this that Rhodri, ancestor of some of today's bearers of the ancient Phillips name, was killed in battle against the Saxon Ceolwulf II of Mercia.

Chapter three:

Invasion and conquest

It was not only Rhodri the Great, celebrated ancestor of bearers of the Phillips name who had to engage in battle against the Vikings.

The first serious shock to Anglo-Saxon control of England came in 789 in the form of sinister black-sailed Viking ships that appeared over the horizon off the island monastery of Lindisfarne, in the northeast of the country.

Lindisfarne was sacked in an orgy of violence and plunder, setting the scene for what would be many more terrifying raids on the coastline of not only England, but also Wales, Ireland and Scotland.

An indication of the terror they brought can be found in one contemporary account of their depredations and desecrations. It laments how 'the pagans desecrated the sanctuaries of God, and poured out the blood of the saints upon the altar, laid waste the house of our hope, trampled on the bodies of saints in the temple of God, like dung in the street.'

But the Vikings, or 'Northmen', in common with the Anglo-Saxons of earlier times, were raiders who eventually stayed – establishing, for example, what became Jorvik, or York, and the trading port of Dublin, in Ireland.

Through intermarriage, the bloodlines of the Anglo-Saxons also became infused with that of the Vikings. Further complicating the genealogical pool, the bloodlines of indigenous Britons such as bearers of the Phillips name, had become mixed with those of the Saxons.

But there would be another infusion of the blood of the 'Northmen' in the wake of the Norman Conquest of 1066 – a key event in English history that sounded the death knell of Anglo-Saxon supremacy.

By 1066, England had become a nation with several powerful competitors to the throne.

In what were extremely complex family, political and military machinations, the English monarch was Harold II, who had succeeded to the throne following the death of Edward the Confessor.

But his right to the throne was contested by two powerful competitors – his brother-in-law King Harold Hardrada of Norway, in alliance with Tostig, Harold II's brother, and Duke William II of Normandy.

In what has become known as The Year of Three Battles, Hardrada invaded England and gained victory over the English king on September 20th at the battle of Fulford, in Yorkshire.

Five days later, however, Harold II decisively defeated his brother-in-law and brother at the battle of Stamford Bridge. But Harold had little time to celebrate his victory, having to immediately march south from Yorkshire to encounter a mighty invasion force, led by Duke William of Normandy that had landed at Hastings, in East Sussex.

Harold's battle-hardened but exhausted force of Anglo-Saxon soldiers confronted the Normans on October 25th in a battle subsequently depicted on the Bayeux tapestry – a 23ft. long strip of embroidered linen thought to have been commissioned eleven years after the event by the Norman Odo of Bayeux.

It was at the top of Senlac Hill that Harold drew up a strong defensive position, building a shield wall to repel Duke William's cavalry and infantry.

The Normans suffered heavy losses, but through a combination of the deadly skill of their archers and the ferocious determination of their cavalry they eventually won the day.

Anglo-Saxon morale had collapsed on the battlefield as word spread through the ranks that Harold had been killed – the Bayeux Tapestry depicting this as having happened when the English king was struck by an arrow to the head. Amidst the carnage of the battlefield, it was difficult to identify Harold – the last of the Anglo-Saxon kings.

Some sources assert William ordered his body to be thrown into the sea, while others state it was secretly buried at Waltham Abbey.

What is known with certainty is that William, in celebration of his great victory, founded Battle Abbey, near the site of the battle, ordering that the altar be sited on the spot where Harold was believed to have fallen.

William was declared King of England on December 25, and what followed was the complete subjugation of his Anglo-Saxon subjects.

Those Normans who had fought on his behalf were rewarded with the lands of Anglo-Saxons, many of whom sought exile abroad as mercenaries.

Within an astonishingly short space of time, Norman manners, customs and law were imposed on England – laying the basis for what subsequently became established 'English' custom and practice.

It was in the aftermath of the Norman Conquest of England that Wales, known in Welsh as *Cymru* from a Brythonic term meaning 'fellow countrymen', and where many bearers of the Phillips name had originally settled from Kent, came under Norman threat. They established a 'frontier region' between England and Wales known as the *Marchia Wallie*, or Welsh Marches. Despite the heroic efforts of great Welsh warrior kings who most notably included Llywelyn ap Gruffydd, Welsh sovereignty was eventually crushed. But it was not until 1536 that a formal Union between the two nations was formalised.

In later centuries, bearers of the name have distinguished themselves in much different bloody arenas of conflict.

Born in 1874 in Cambria, California, Reuben Phillips was a recipient of the Medal of Honor – America's highest award for military valour – for his actions as a corporal in the United States Marine Corps during the 1898 to 1901 Boxer Rebellion in China.

Phillips, who died in 1936, received the Medal of Honor for his bravery in action on two separate occasions in June of 1900.

Taking to the skies, Samuel Phillips was the highly decorated U.S. Air Force general who served as a combat pilot with the 364th Fighter Group of the Eighth Air Force during the Second World War.

Born in 1921 in Springerville, Arizona, he further distinguished himself after the war by serving from 1964 to 1969 as Director of NASA's Apollo Manned Lunar Landing Program and, from 1972 to 1973, as director of the space agency.

Also from 1973 to 1975 the commander of Air Force Systems Command (COMAFSC), he died in 1990 – the recipient of an impressive list of awards that include two Distinguished Flying Crosses, the Air Force Distinguished Service Medal and two NASA Distinguished Service Medals.

From the battlefield to the world of politics, Wendell Phillips was the noted American activist of the nineteenth century famed for his oratorical skills. Born in Boston in 1811, the lawyer and abolitionist joined the American Anti-Slavery Society in 1836 and, touring and lecturing extensively throughout the United States, became known as "abolition's golden trumpet."

Also an advocate of equal rights for Native Americans and women and for universal suffrage, he died in 1884. He is remembered today not only through a monument to him in Boston Public Garden, but also through a number of sayings that include:

What gunpowder has done for war, the printing press has done for the mind; Eternal vigilance is the price of liberty and *The best education in the world is that got by struggling to get a living*.

Chapter four:

On the world stage

Bearers of the Phillips name, in a variety of its spellings, have gained international celebrity status.

The main songwriter and leader of the band the Mamas and Papas, **John Phillips** was the American musician born in 1935.

It was throughout the 1960s that Phillips, along with fellow band members Cass Elliot, Denny Doherty and his wife **Michelle Phillips**, enjoyed a string of major hits that include *California Dreamin'*, *Monday, Monday* and *I Saw Her Again*.

Phillips, who died in 2001, also wrote *San Francisco (Be Sure to Wear Flowers in Your Hair)*, the hit song performed by his friend Scott McKenzie that became the 'anthem' for the 1967 'Summer of Love' in San Francisco.

The Mamas and Papas song *California Dreamin'* was co-written with his second wife Michelle, born Holly Michelle Gilliam in 1944 in Long Beach, California. The singer, songwriter and actress describes the song, which still nets her substantial royalties, as "the best wake-up call ever."

She had been asleep in a New York hotel room when her husband woke her up to help complete the song he had been working on throughout the night.

The couple divorced in 1970, and she was later married for a brief period of only eight days to the actor Dennis Hopper.

Inducted along with her band-mates into both the Rock and Roll Hall of Fame and the Vocal Group Hall of Fame, she has also enjoyed success in film and television series that include *Knots Landing* and *Beverley Hills 90210*.

Through John Phillips, she is the mother of the singer and actress **Chynna Phillips**, born Gilliam Chynna Phillips in 1968 in Los Angeles.

As a member of the band Wilson Phillips she had success with albums that include the 1990 *Wilson Phillips* and also with her 1995 solo album *Naked and Sacred*. Married to the actor William Baldwin since 1991, she has also appeared in films that include the 1987 *Some Kind of Wonderful* and, from 1989, *Say Anything*.

She is a half-sister of the actress, model and singer **Bijou Phillips**, through John Phillips' third marriage to the South African actress, model and artist Geneviève Waite.

Born in 1980 in Greenwich, Fairfield County, Connecticut, her debut album was the 1999 *I'd Rather Eat Glass*, while her film credits include the 1999 *Black and White* and the 2008 *Choke*.

She is also a half-sister of the actress and singer **Mackenzie Phillips**, through her father's first marriage.

Born in 1959 in Alexandra, Virginia, she is best known for her role in the 1973 *American Graffiti*, while her role in the 2010 *Peach Plum Pear* won her an Honorary Best Actress Award at the Female Eye Film Festival in Toronto.

Not only a poet and folk musician but also a labour organiser, **Utah Phillips**, born Bruce Duncan Phillips in 1935 in Cleveland, Ohio, was known as "the Golden Voice of the Great Southwest."

A promoter through his music and poetry early in his career of the aims and ideals of the Industrial Workers of the World – better known as the Wobblies – his albums include the 1975 *El Capitan* and, released three years before his death in 2008, *Starlight on the Rails*.

Also in music, **Herbie Phillips**, born in 1935 in Lincoln, Nebraska and who died in 1995, was the American jazz trumpeter, big band composer and arranger who worked for artists who included the Buddy Rich Big Band and Frank Sinatra.

Back to the stage, **Ethan Phillips** is the American actor best known for television roles that include that of Neelix, from 1995 to 2001, in *Star Trek: Voyager*, and also roles in *Benson*, *Boston Legal* and *The Mentalist*.

Born in 1955 in Garden City, New York, his film credits include the 1986 *Critters* and the 1990 *Green Card*.

A creative consultant from 1964 to 1969 on the American television drama series *Peyton Place*, **Irna Phillips** was the radio and television creator and scriptwriter born in 1901 in Chicago.

Creator of popular American radio series that included the 1930 to 1932 *Painted Dreams*, she also created television dramas that include, from 1967 until her death in 1973, *Love is a Many Splendored Thing*.

Born in 1986 in Sutton Coldfield, Birmingham, **James** and **Oliver Phelps** are the English twin brothers and actors best known for their roles as Fred and George Weasley in the *Harry Potter* series of films.

Back across the Atlantic, **Emo Philips**, born in 1956 in Chicago, is the American comedian and entertainer famous for his falsetto tone of voice.

In addition to his career as a stand-up comedian, he has also appeared in films that include the 1992 *Meet the Parents* and the 1998 *Desperation Boulevard*.

Bearers of the Phillips name, in a variety of its spelling forms, have also excelled in the highly competitive world of sport.

A member of the British three day event team that won the gold medal at the 1972 Munich Olympics, **Captain Mark Phillips** is the champion equestrian and former soldier who was married from 1973 to 1992 to Princess Anne.

Born in 1948, he is the father through his marriage to the Princess Royal of the equestrian **Zara Phillips**.

Born in 1981 in Paddington, London and 13th in the line of succession to the throne, she was the winner of the Eventing World Championship at Aachen in 2006 and was also a member of the British team that won the silver medal at the 2012 Olympics in London.

Voted the 2006 BBC Sports Personality of the Year, she married England rugby union player Mike Tindall in 2010.

In the much different sport of basketball,

Rashad Phillips, born in Detroit in 1978, is the American former player who, in a career lasting from 2001 to 2009, competed in more than eight countries for more than ten different teams.

In gymnastics, **Jacyie Lyn Phelps**, born in 1979 in Indianapolis, is the American gymnast who was a member of her country's Olympic gold medal-winning women's team at the 1996 Olympics in Atlanta.

From sport to the often cut-throat world of politics, **Sir Robert Philp**, born in Glasgow in 1851 and who died in 1922, rose to serve as Premier of Queensland from 1899 to 1903 after emigrating from Scotland to Australia with his family when he was aged 12

Born in 1914 near Dannevirke, New Zealand, **William Phillips** was one of the twentieth century's most influential economists.

A trained engineer in addition to economist, he is best known for the publication in 1958 of a pioneering work on the relationship between inflation and unemployment, illustrated by what is now known as the Phillips Curve; he died in 1975.

In the field of electronics, **Anton Frederik Philips**, born in 1874 in Gelderland, Netherlands was, along with his brother Gerard Philips, the founder in 1912 of the Dutch electronics company Philips.

He died in 1951, while his son **Frits Philips**, born in Eindhoven in 1905, is honoured for having saved the lives of more than 380 Jews during the Second World War when German troops occupied the Netherlands.

By claiming that they were indispensable as workers in his factory, he helped them evade deportation to the death camps.

It was in recognition of this that in 1996 Israel honoured him as "Righteous Among Nations"; he died in 2005, aged 100.

In the creative world of art, **Sir Robert Philipson**, born in 1916 in Broughton-in-Furness, Lancashire was famous for his work in the Scottish arts scene.

Moving over the border to the Scottish town of Dumfries with his family when he was aged 14, he later studied at Edinburgh College of Art, teaching drawing and painting there from 1960 to 1982.

A member of the Edinburgh School group of artists, he is particularly known for his cockfight paintings and his 1960 painting *Cathedral*.

President of the Royal Scottish Academy

from 1973 to 1983 and knighted in 1976 for his services to art in Scotland, he died in 1992.

A self-taught portrait painter whose identity as an artist remained largely unknown in his lifetime, **Ammi Phillips** was born in 1788 in Colebrook, Connecticut.

He died in 1865, but it was not until 1924 that a stunning collection of unsigned portraits went on display at an antiques show in Kent, New England.

Not knowing the artist's identity, he was simply named 'the Kent Limner', while in 1940 another collection was found in New England.

It was only in1968 that Ammi Phillips was identified as the painter of both collections, while by 1976 about 400 paintings in total had been attributed to him.

Now recognised as one of the most prolific American folk artists of all time, his work was featured on a U.S. postage stamp in 1998.

Two particularly inventive bearers of the Phillips name were the British aviation pioneer **Horatio Phillips** and the American engineer **Henry F. Phillips**.

Born in 1845 in Streatham, London, Horatio Phillips pioneered aerofoil design, devising a wind tunnel to study varieties of aerofoil shapes and provide lift; he died in 1924.

Indispensable to any toolbox, be it in the factory or the home, is the 'crosshead' screwdriver known as the Phillips screwdriver – invented by the American engineer and businessman Henry F. Phillips, born in 1895.

It was in the early 1930s that fellow engineer John P. Thompson sold Phillips a basic design for a crosshead screw – one which Phillips radically re-designed in addition to inventing the crosshead screwdriver.

Forming the Phillips Screw Company in 1934, one of his first customers was General Motors for use on its Cadillac assembly lines.

Phillips died in 1958, by which time more than 85% of American tool manufacturers had a license for the Phillips design.